COMPLETE PATTERNS AND INSTRUCTIONS

SCROLL SAW
TOYS
AND VEHICLES

Functional designs for contemporary interests by Stan Graves

FOX BOOKS
Fox Chapel Publishing Co Inc.

1999 by Fox Chapel Publishing Company, Inc.

Publisher:	Alan Giagnocavo
Project Editor:	Ayleen Stellhorn
Design, text, production,cover photo:	Stan Graves
Studio photography:	Larry Volbruck

ISBN 1-56523-115-5

Scrollsaw Toys and Vehicles by Stan Graves is a first-time effort for the author. This is a new publication by Fox Chapel Publishing Company, Inc. All rights reserved. No part of this publication may be reproduced, stored in a retrieval system, or transmitted in any form or by any means, electronic, mechanical, photocopying, recording or otherwise, without prior written permission of the publisher. The patterns in this book are copyrighted by the author. Scrollers may use these patterns to create their own products for sale, but the patterns themselves may not be duplicated for resale or distributed in any form.

It is intended that the toys featured in this book can be made for play or display. The instructions will suggest varied finishing techniques from which the hobbiest can choose. The idea was to develop vehicles with style and function that fit contemporary interests and, at the same time, could be constructed with common, easy-to-find materials.

We wish to thank Alan Giagnocavo and his staff at Fox Chapel Publishing Company,Inc. Without his confidence this book could not have been published.

The author also offers pattern designs on other subjects, such as trees, wild and domestic animals, and plants. For information send $1.00 to Stan Graves, 900 23rd Ave., Moline, IL 61265.

To order a copy of this book,
please send check or money order
for $12.95 plus $2.50 shipping to:
Fox Chapel Book Orders
1970 Broad Street
East Petersburg, PA 17250
1–800–457–9112

Try your favorite supplier first!

CONTENTS

Please note: Because of design improvements after prototype models were built and photographed, readers may notice variations between patterns and photos in this book.

INSTRUCTIONS

SCROLLSAWS AND OTHER POWER TOOLS

If you are new at scrollsawing or are interested in getting started, a little introductory education will serve you well when it's time to purchase tools and supplies. There is a nice selection of books written on scrollsaws offered by hobby shops specializing in wood working. Some home centers also carry books. Specialty shops can help you locate shows where manufacturers demonstrate their products and will let you try them out. Some dealers may offer limited demo periods. It doesn't hurt to ask. Research can be very enjoyable. You will begin to learn details such as proper blade selection and the importance of attaching and detaching blades during operation. While doing my research it became apparent I didn't need an expensive saw to match my needs. As you advance, you will be in a better position to judge when it's time to purchase a more substantial tool.

A drillpress is a must for drilling holes for axles and other pinning that requires exacting perpendicular drilling. You'll find reasonably priced models that are adequate for light work such as these toys. Similar possibilities apply to disk sanders mounted to stationary tables. A versatile tool to own is a sander that has a sanding disk plus a one inch wide sanding belt simultaneously powered by a single electric motor.

It is very gratifying to feel you've purchased the proper tools, and then allotted plenty of time to follow instructions for setup and safe operation. If you prefer to set up without reading instructions it's almost guaranteed you may miss important pointers. After all, the manufacturer knows his product better than anyone.

REFINEMENTS

You may choose to add refinements beyond the basic functional toy. A 1/8" round-over on all outside edges adds a consistent, finished look and feel and a safe edge for little hands. I use a router attached to a small table. The router, table, and 1/8" round-over bit are available at most stores that sell power tools. I also have a 1/8" round-over for my high-speed Dremel® Moto-Flex tool. Dremel offers a small table with a clamping device that lets you create a "tiny router table." The small size enables one to round corners with very tight turns.

FINISHING

I painted some of my vehicle prototypes to get a feel for how they look. My preference is leaving them natural with black accents. But if you prefer to paint your toy, there's a decision you'll need to make about the quality of the paint job. For a nice high-gloss finish you'll need to work for it. First, discuss your project with a knowledgeable paint dealer. Purchase an aerosol primer sanding sealer and a glossy oil-base aerosol in the color of your choice, 150 and 220 grit sandpaper and fine-grade steel wool. Before assembly, sand each part with 150 and 220. Spread newspapers in a well ventilated area and place each part to be painted on a scrap of wood. Spray with a light coat of primer, then sand with 220 after each coat. Be sure to let each

INSTRUCTIONS Cont.

coat dry thoroughly after sanding. Repeat the same process with with your chosen color. Now, use only 220 paper and steel wool. Don't worry about sanding through to the primer. Now, the tricky part. After the third coat is dried thoroughly and rubbed lightly with steel wool, hold or clamp a light beyond the piece to be painted until you see reflection off the top surface to be painted. Quickly spray on a nice thick coat at all angles until the paint is thick enough that the droplets run together. The light reflection will enable you to observe this. If you try to touch up after the paint starts to set, which is only a few seconds, the droplets will not blend with the original coat. This will leave a dull blend. I would suggest practicing on scrap material.

MATERIALS

Nearly all common, usually found in local home centers. Look to see if they have a bargain bin where damaged prime-quality pine boards are offered at a reduced price. The two exceptions are Baltic plywood, 1/4" and 1/2", 1/4" and 3/8" axle end caps. I get them from a store that supplies products for most woodworking hobbies: The Woodcraft Shop Bettendorf, IA 319 359-9684.

- 3/4" PINE
- 1/8", 1/4", 1/2" BALTIC PLYWOOD
- 1/2",3/8",1/4" DOWEL RODS
- 3/8" END CAPS
- 1/4" END CAPS
- CARPENTERS GLUE
- GELLED SUPER GLUE*
- SPRAY GLUE
- 1/4" ELASTIC BAND
- SMALL-HEAD DRYWALL SCREWS
- 1" and 1/2" BRADS

BEGINNING TIPS

It's important to follow the instructions in sequence while building these toys. For example, it's easier and safer to drill the axle holes in a large block of wood than it is after the vehicle body is cut out. All patterns in this book utilize the following techniques: 1. Select materials. 2. Spread carpenters glue, join and clamp blocks together. Let dry.   3. Transfer patterns with carbon paper or make a copy and tack it on the block surface with spray glue.
4. Drill any holes for axles or pegs. Brad-point bits work fine. I prefer Forstner bits for clean cutting. 5. Cut out pieces. 6. Round edges if desired. Dotted lines on patterns indicate objects that appear behind those that are closer. This guide to assembly sequence applies to each pattern where appropriate throughout this book.

*I use the gelled version of super glue by Loctight® which is a nice thick consistancy and sets up very slowly until the two surfaces to be glued are pushed together. Strong adhesion is permanent in about five seconds, so you must be organized. Because of its great holding power it can be applied in small amounts so there's no squeeze out that looks unsightly.

LET'S MAKE WHEELS

1. Select wood and determine wheel size.
2. With a compass, draw three circles on plywood: One at final wheel size, a second slightly larger, and a third about half way to center. See Fig. 1.
3. With two 1/2" brads, tack plywood to a 3/4"pine block. Leave brads part way out for removal later.
4. Drill holes for axles.
5. Cut out wheel on outside circle.(2)
6. Gently remove plywood from 3/4" block. (I use the edge of a wood chisel.)
7. Cut out center circle from plywood, Fig.2.Round-off inside edge and sand.
8. If you choose to add the black accent inside the circle, Fig. 3, you may use paint. I use vinal adhesive-backed shelf liner by Rubbermaid[R]. Hardware stores usually carry it.
9. Add carpenters glue near outside edge of plywood ring. Tack ring to 3/4" pine wheel. Any glue that squeezes out will be sanded off in the process explained next.
10. For setting up jig see illustration below.

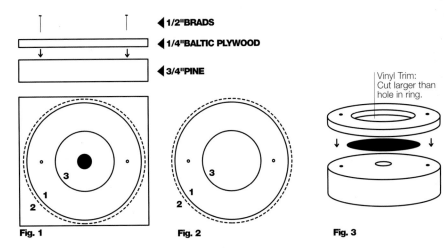

1/2"BRADS
1/4"BALTIC PLYWOOD
3/4"PINE

Vinyl Trim: Cut larger than hole in ring.

Fig. 1   Fig. 2   Fig. 3

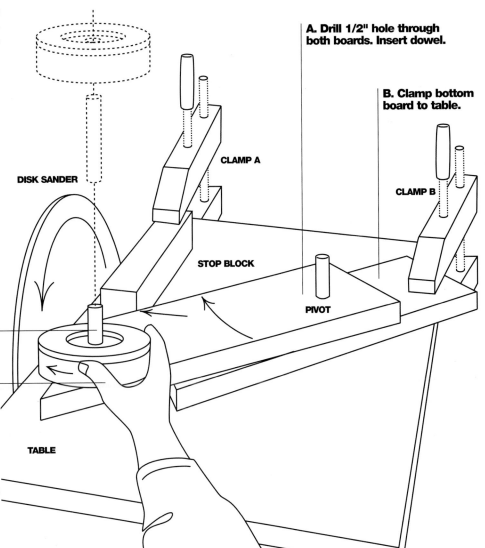

A. Drill 1/2" hole through both boards. Insert dowel.

B. Clamp bottom board to table.

CLAMP A

CLAMP B

DISK SANDER

STOP BLOCK

PIVOT

C. Drill 3/8"hole in top board located so wheel will overlap end of board.

D. Set wheel with 3/8" dowel.

E. Before turning on sander, pivot wheel over to sanding disk. Adjust stop block with clamp-A. Pivot wheel away and turn on sander. With a firm grip carefully move to and turn wheel against sander until it's sanded down to the second circle (final wheel size). But first, for ease and safety, I suggest removing small amounts at a time by adjusting the stop block 2 or 3 times. (Clamp A.)

To make all wheels exactly the same size, strike a mark on the table so you can accurately return the stop-block to that point for each wheel.

TABLE

See page 40 for information on how to order ready-made wheels.

MACHO PICKUP

LITTLE MUDDER ABOARD GOOSE-NECK TRAILER

TOP LEFT
Goose-neck trailer in loading position.

LEFT
**Platform pinned in position for transport.
Bungee cable secures ATV onto trailer.
See cable holding hitch in place.**

LITTLE MUDDER

ABOARD GOOSE-NECK TRAILER

See pages 1-2 for instructions and a general discussion on appropriate materials and finishing. Pages 6-7, "Macho Pickup," are set up to help with the sequence of construction. Shaded areas suggest black color.

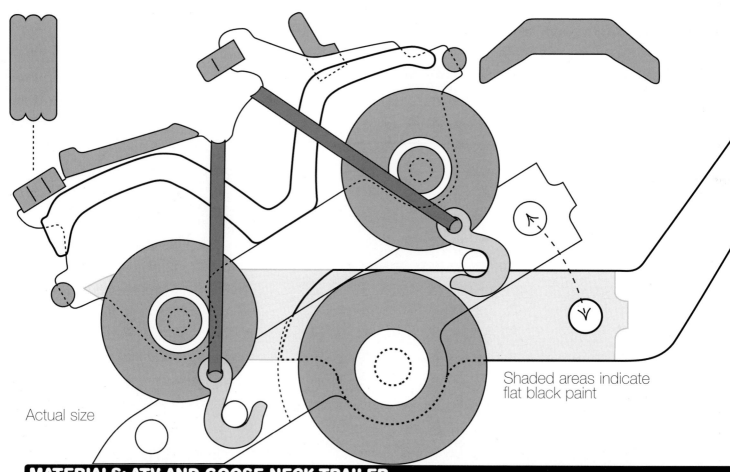

Actual size

Shaded areas indicate flat black paint

MATERIALS: ATV AND GOOSE-NECK TRAILER

1. 3/4" PINE
2. 1/4" BALTIC PLYWOOD
3. 3/8" DOWEL
4. 3/16" DOWEL
5. 1/4" DOWEL
6. 3/8" END CAPS
7. 1/4" END CAPS
8. 1/4" ELASTIC BAND
9. FLAT BLACK PAINT
10. CARPENTERS GLUE
11. GELLED SUPER GLUE

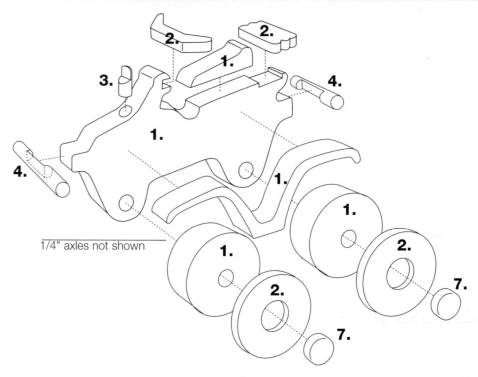

1/4" axles not shown

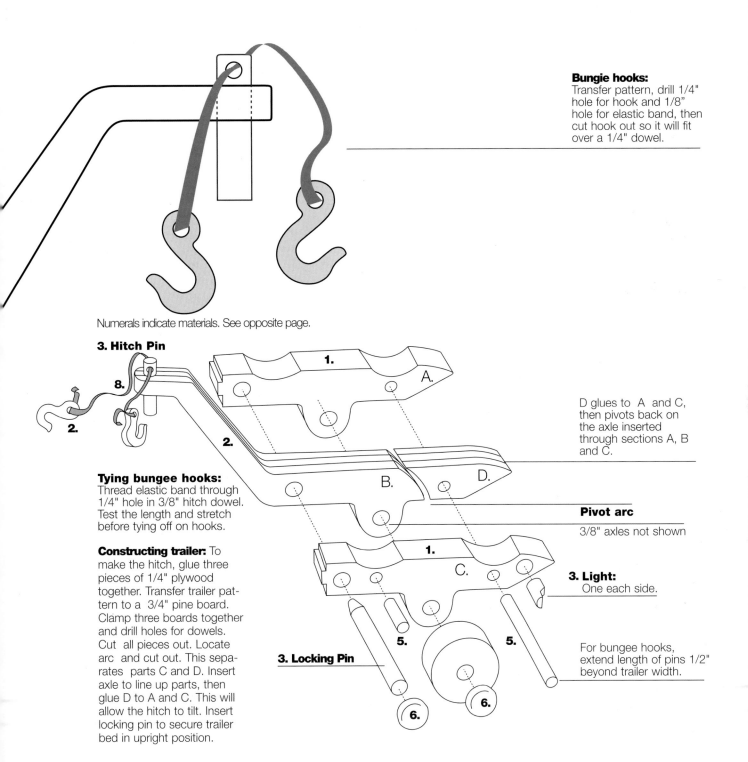

Bungie hooks:
Transfer pattern, drill 1/4"
hole for hook and 1/8"
hole for elastic band, then
cut hook out so it will fit
over a 1/4" dowel.

Numerals indicate materials. See opposite page.

3. Hitch Pin

8.

2.

1.

A.

2.

D glues to A and C,
then pivots back on
the axle inserted
through sections A, B
and C.

B.

D.

Tying bungee hooks:
Thread elastic band through
1/4" hole in 3/8" hitch dowel.
Test the length and stretch
before tying off on hooks.

Pivot arc

3/8" axles not shown

1.

C.

Constructing trailer: To
make the hitch, glue three
pieces of 1/4" plywood
together. Transfer trailer pattern to a 3/4" pine board.
Clamp three boards together
and drill holes for dowels.
Cut all pieces out. Locate
arc and cut out. This sepa-
rates parts C and D. Insert
axle to line up parts, then
glue D to A and C. This will
allow the hitch to tilt. Insert
locking pin to secure trailer
bed in upright position.

3. Light:
One each side.

5.

5.

For bungee hooks,
extend length of pins 1/2"
beyond trailer width.

3. Locking Pin

6.

6.

11

HI-RIDE SPORTS UTILITY

HI-RIDE SPORTS UTILITY

The Sports Utility is virtually the same as the Macho Pickup with exception of the rear profile and the hitch design. Note how the area behind the back wheels is squared off to accommodate the hitch piece.

See pages 1-2 for instructions and a general discussion on materials and finishing. Pages 6-7, "Macho Pickup," are set up to help with the sequence of construction. Shaded areas suggest black color.

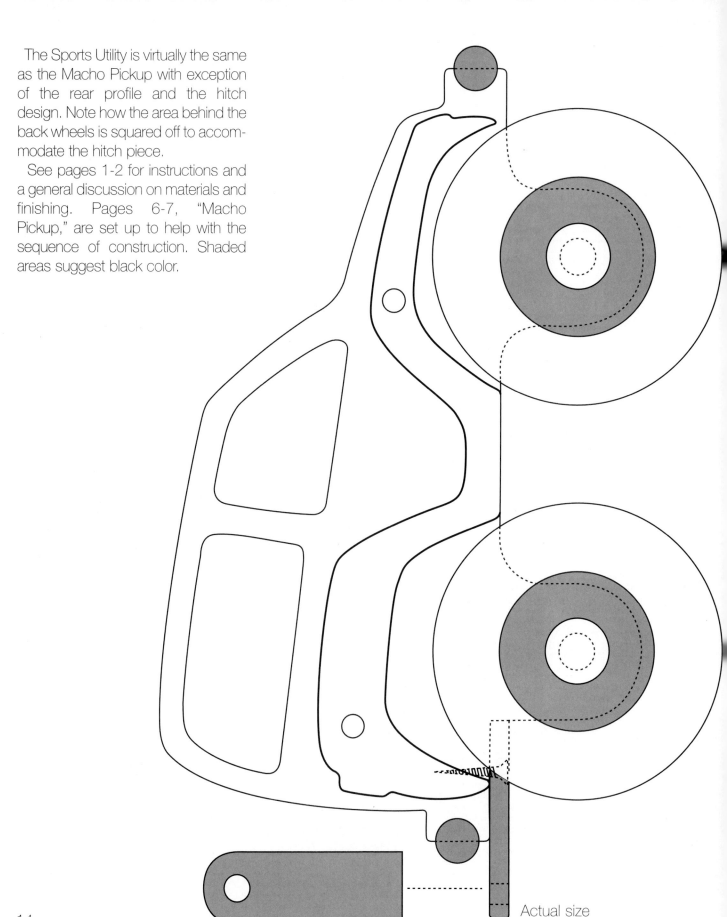

Actual size

MATERIALS: HI-RIDE SPORTS UTILITY

1. 3/4" PINE
2. 1/4" BALTIC PLYWOOD
3. 1/2" DOWEL
4. 3/8" DOWEL
5. 1/4" DOWEL
6. 3/8" END CAPS
7. FLAT BLACK PAINT
8. CARPENTERS GLUE
9. GELLED SUPER GLUE

1. Two pieces glued together with carpenters glue.

4. 3/8"axles not shown

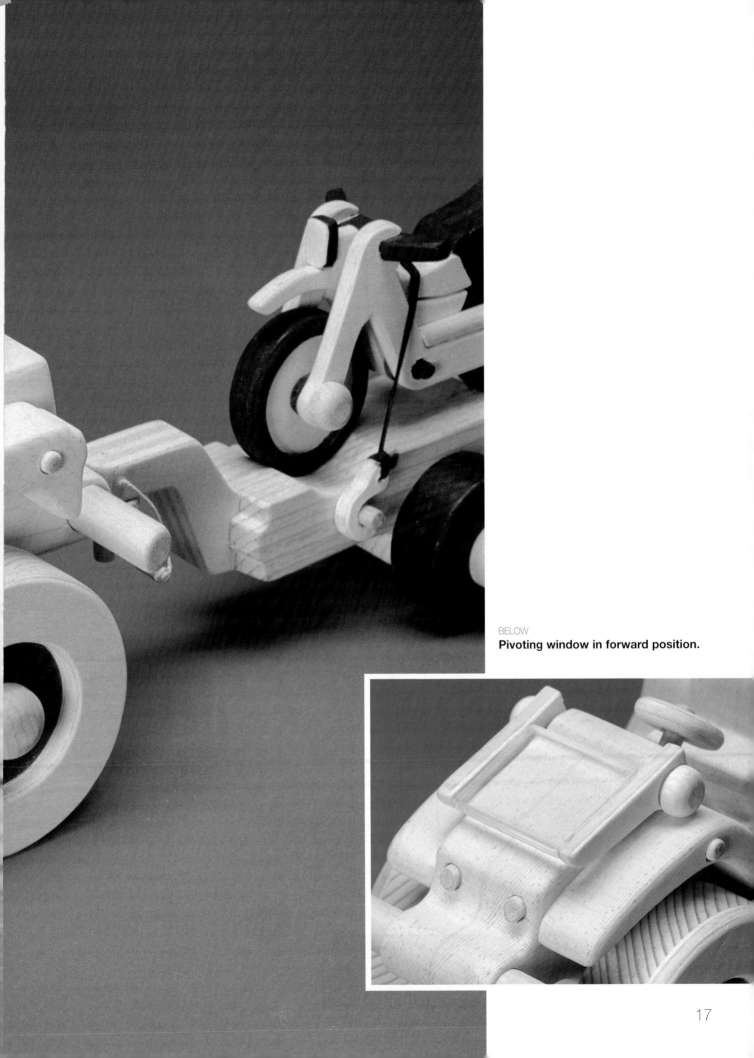

BELOW
Pivoting window in forward position.

**Bike is held secure by bungee cables
and concave cutouts in trailer.**

**Hitch pin keeps trailer from
releasing during transport.**

DIRT BIKE ON TRAILER

Actual size

The dirt bike is almost totally made up of 1/4" Baltic plywood. It's wheels have 1/8" plywood rings.

The trailer is similar to the goose-neck, pages 10-11, except that the center pivot has been eliminated.

A bumper hitch attaches to the leading edge for hookup to the jeep or sports utility vehicles. Of course, the pickup could be made with a low hitch also.

See pages 1-2 and 6-7 for more information on technique.

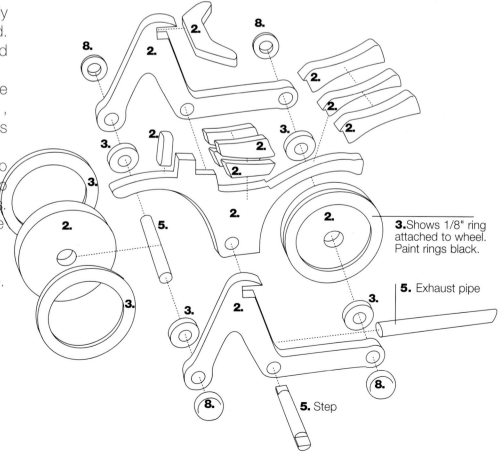

3. Shows 1/8" ring attached to wheel. Paint rings black.

5. Exhaust pipe

5. Step

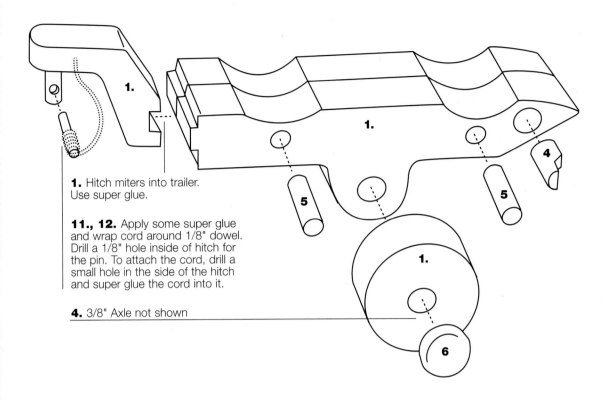

1. Hitch miters into trailer. Use super glue.

11., 12. Apply some super glue and wrap cord around 1/8" dowel. Drill a 1/8" hole inside of hitch for the pin. To attach the cord, drill a small hole in the side of the hitch and super glue the cord into it.

4. 3/8" Axle not shown

MATERIALS: DIRT BIKE ON TRAILER

1. 3/4" PINE
2. 1/4" PLYWOOD
3. 1/8" PLYWOOD
4. 3/8" DOWEL
5. 1/4" DOWEL
6. 1/8" DOWEL
7. 3/8" END CAPS
8. 1/4" END CAPS
9. FLAT BLACK PAINT
10. CARPENTERS GLUE
11. GELLED SUPER GLUE
12. SMALL CORD

SEMI LOW-BOY HAULER

Loading ramp at rear
of trailer rotates from transport
to loading position.

Bungee cables store on rods
when trailer has no load

Dowel rods in low-boy trailer are spaced for wheelbase on tractor, lower ramp, and for pickup, upper ramp. Rods can be adjusted for convenient bungee cable hook-up.

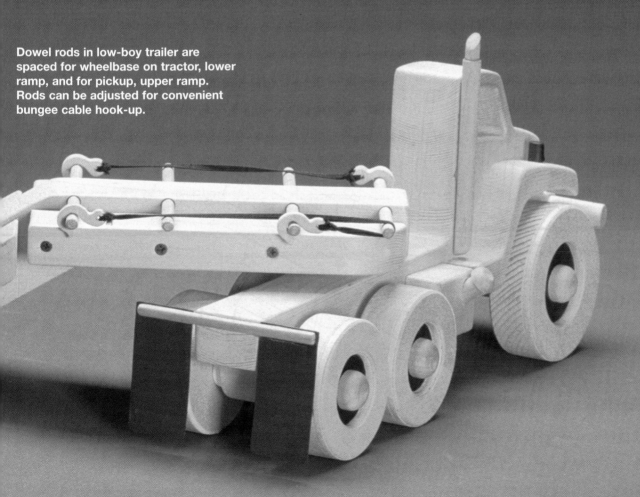

ARTICULATED END-LOADER

ABOVE
**Pin locks bucket in transport position.
Removes for material loading.**

LEFT
**End-loader is secured by bungee cables
stretched over machine and dowel rods
extending through trailer bed.**

To make the articulated end-loader a decision must be made to build or not to build in the articulated steering feature. If not, the project could be simplified considerably. I think it really adds a special dimension to the toy. Especially when you hold and work with it.

Because the steering mechanism is the same as the

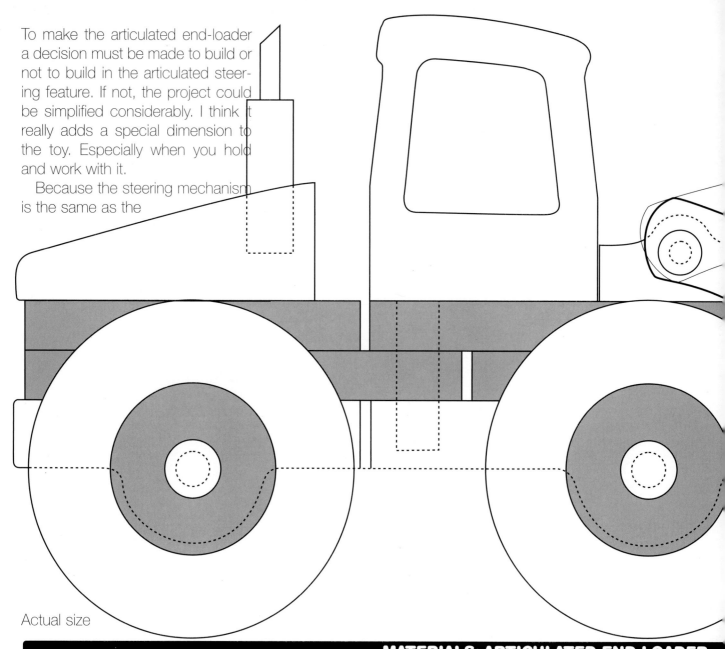

Actual size

ag tractor on pages 34-35, refer to those pages for details on the "top view" pattern.

For making wheels, follow instructions on page 3. Add an extra 1/4" ring to the inside of the wheel to give it more size. There will be a need for three 1/4" spacers on the inside of each wheel to give the machine a nice stable look. Make the loader before the bucket. The width of the bucket is the same measure as the wheels installed with spacers.

MATERIALS: ARTICULATED END LOADER

1. 3/4" PINE
2. 1/2" BALTIC PLYWOOD
3. 1/4" BALTIC PLYWOOD
4. 1/2" DOWEL
5. 3/8" DOWEL
6. 1/4" DOWEL
7. 3/8" END CAPS
8. 1/4" END CAPS
9. FLAT BLACK PAINT
10. 1/2" BRADS
11. CARPENTERS GLUE
12. GELLED SUPER GLUE

ARTICULATED
END-LOADER

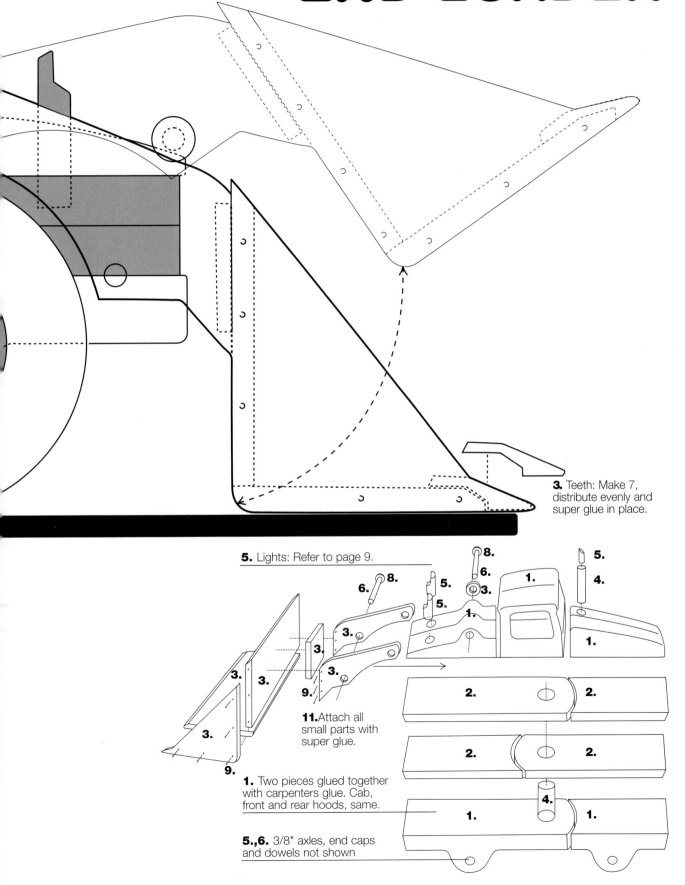

3. Teeth: Make 7, distribute evenly and super glue in place.

5. Lights: Refer to page 9.

11. Attach all small parts with super glue.

1. Two pieces glued together with carpenters glue. Cab, front and rear hoods, same.

5.,6. 3/8" axles, end caps and dowels not shown

Tractor steers by center articulation.

Hitch pin secures trailing implement.

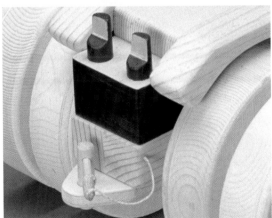

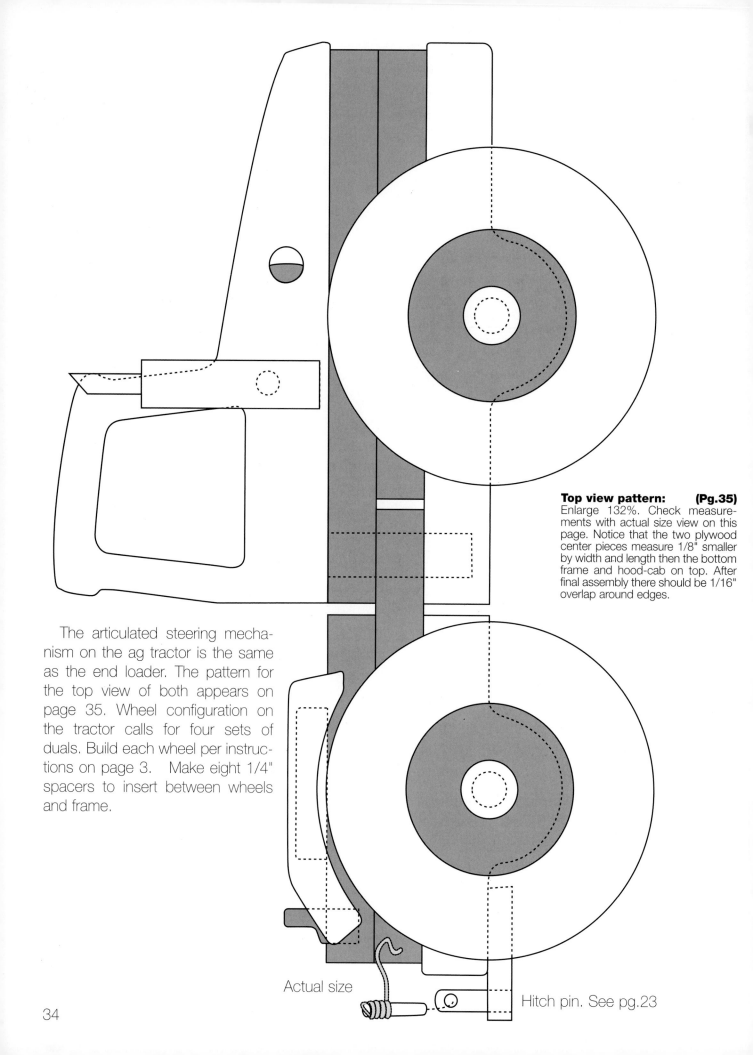

Top view pattern: **(Pg.35)**
Enlarge 132%. Check measurements with actual size view on this page. Notice that the two plywood center pieces measure 1/8" smaller by width and length then the bottom frame and hood-cab on top. After final assembly there should be 1/16" overlap around edges.

The articulated steering mechanism on the ag tractor is the same as the end loader. The pattern for the top view of both appears on page 35. Wheel configuration on the tractor calls for four sets of duals. Build each wheel per instructions on page 3. Make eight 1/4" spacers to insert between wheels and frame.

Actual size

Hitch pin. See pg.23

ARTICULATED AG TRACTOR

MATERIALS: ARTICULATED AG TRACTOR

1. 3/4" PINE
2. 1/2" BALTIC PLYWOOD
3. 1/4" BALTIC PLYWOOD
4. 1/2" DOWEL
5. 3/8" DOWEL
6. 1/4" DOWEL
7. 3/8" END CAPS
8. 1/4" END CAPS
9. FLAT BLACK PAINT
10. 1/2" and 1" BRADS
11. CARPENTERS GLUE
12. GELLED SUPER GLUE

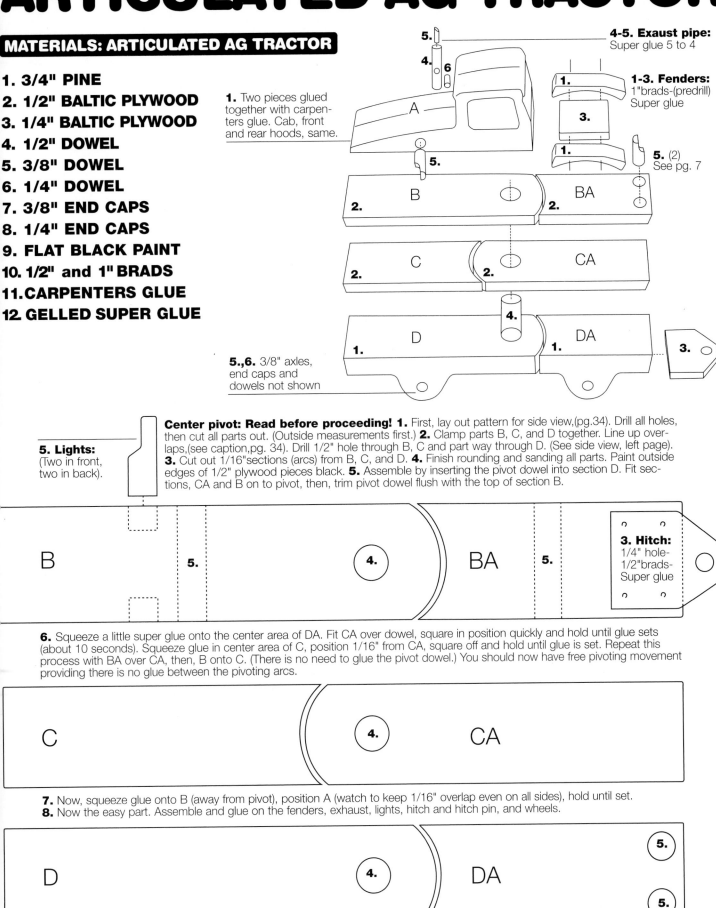

1. Two pieces glued together with carpenters glue. Cab, front and rear hoods, same.

4-5. Exaust pipe: Super glue 5 to 4

1-3. Fenders: 1"brads-(predrill) Super glue

5. (2) See pg. 7

2.

5.,6. 3/8" axles, end caps and dowels not shown

5. Lights: (Two in front, two in back).

Center pivot: Read before proceeding! 1. First, lay out pattern for side view,(pg.34). Drill all holes, then cut all parts out. (Outside measurements first.) **2.** Clamp parts B, C, and D together. Line up overlaps,(see caption,pg. 34). Drill 1/2" hole through B, C and part way through D. (See side view, left page). **3.** Cut out 1/16"sections (arcs) from B, C, and D. **4.** Finish rounding and sanding all parts. Paint outside edges of 1/2" plywood pieces black. **5.** Assemble by inserting the pivot dowel into section D. Fit sections, CA and B on to pivot, then, trim pivot dowel flush with the top of section B.

B **5.** **4.** **BA** **5.**

3. Hitch: 1/4" hole- 1/2"brads- Super glue

6. Squeeze a little super glue onto the center area of DA. Fit CA over dowel, square in position quickly and hold until glue sets (about 10 seconds). Squeeze glue in center area of C, position 1/16" from CA, square off and hold until glue is set. Repeat this process with BA over CA, then, B onto C. (There is no need to glue the pivot dowel.) You should now have free pivoting movement providing there is no glue between the pivoting arcs.

C **4.** **CA**

7. Now, squeeze glue onto B (away from pivot), position A (watch to keep 1/16" overlap even on all sides), hold until set.
8. Now the easy part. Assemble and glue on the fenders, exhaust, lights, hitch and hitch pin, and wheels.

D **4.** **DA** **5.** **5.**

Enlarge 132%

FOLDING CHISEL PLOW

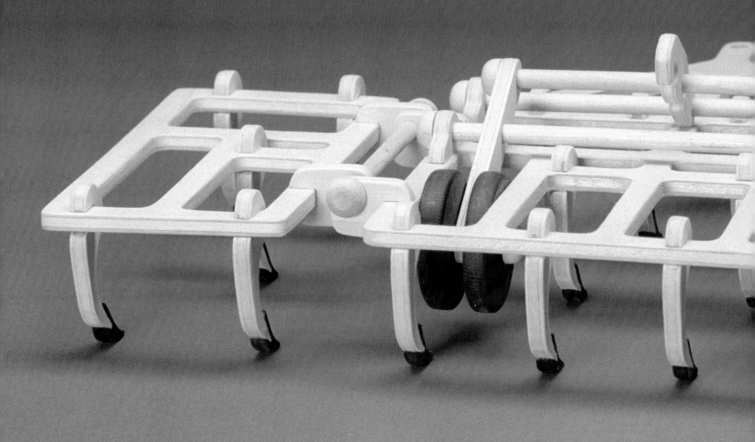

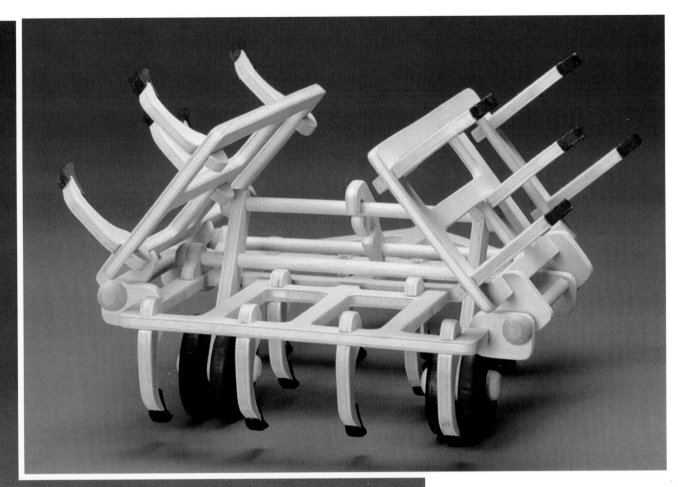

For transport, wings fold up and wheels lock down.

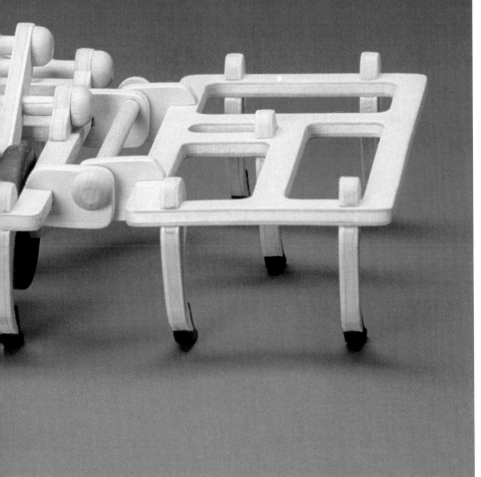

For cultivating, wings fold down and wheels lock in raised position.

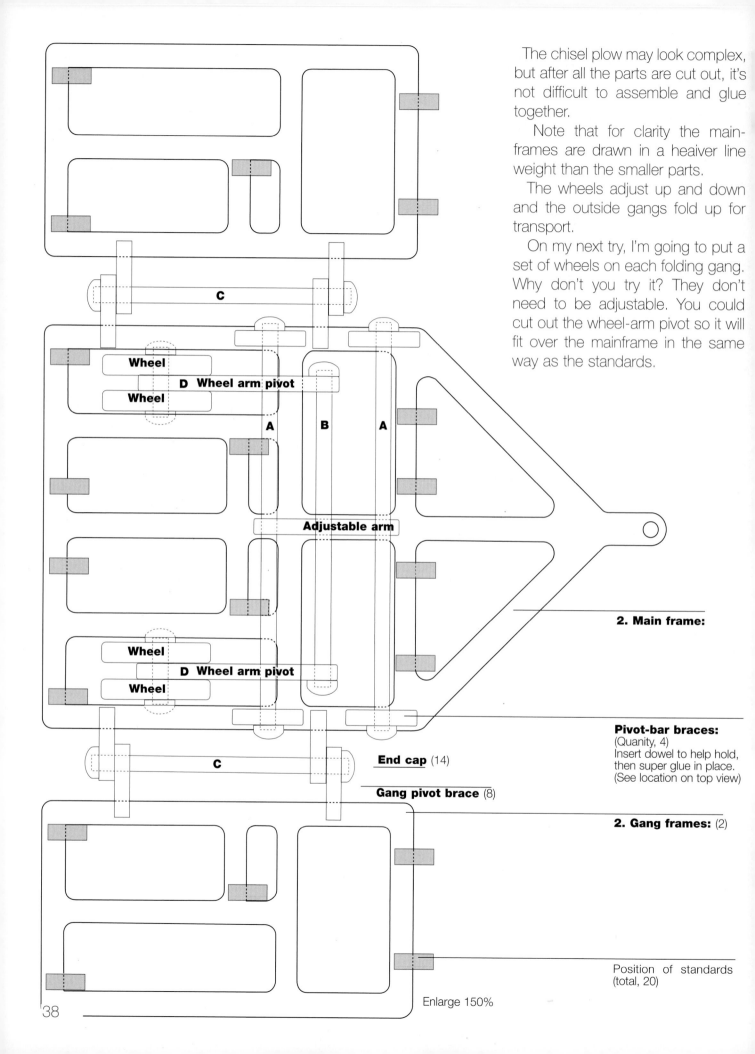

The chisel plow may look complex, but after all the parts are cut out, it's not difficult to assemble and glue together.

Note that for clarity the main-frames are drawn in a heaiver line weight than the smaller parts.

The wheels adjust up and down and the outside gangs fold up for transport.

On my next try, I'm going to put a set of wheels on each folding gang. Why don't you try it? They don't need to be adjustable. You could cut out the wheel-arm pivot so it will fit over the mainframe in the same way as the standards.

C

Wheel

D Wheel arm pivot

Wheel

A   **B**   **A**

Adjustable arm

2. Main frame:

Wheel

D Wheel arm pivot

Wheel

C

End cap (14)

Gang pivot brace (8)

Pivot-bar braces:
(Quanity, 4)
Insert dowel to help hold, then super glue in place.
(See location on top view)

2. Gang frames: (2)

Position of standards
(total, 20)

Enlarge 150%

FOLDING CHISEL PLOW

MATERIALS: FOLDING CHISEL PLOW

1. 3/4" PINE: (Wheels only.) Make two wheels from 3/4" pine , then cut each down the center, lengthwise. Sand and finish the four 3/8" wheels.

2. 1/4" BALTIC PLYWOOD: The plow will be too delicate for a child. You could use 3/8" Baltic plywood.

3. 1/4" DOWELS: After enlargenent, the pattern below shows actual length of dowels.

4. 1/4" END CAPS: Quanity:(14) Remember, drill all holes before cutting out pieces.

5. FLAT BLACK PAINT

6. CARPENTERS GLUE

7. GELLED SUPER GLUE

How to make chisel standards: (Quanity, 20)
    You may want to cut out more than one at a time by stacking. Stack as many as you're comfortable with and cut out the whole standard, including the point at the bottom. Then cut the points off. (Dark area on side view.) Paint the points black and super glue them back onto the standards.

Enlarge 168%. For accuracy, check length of gang with top view of pattern after enlargements are made.

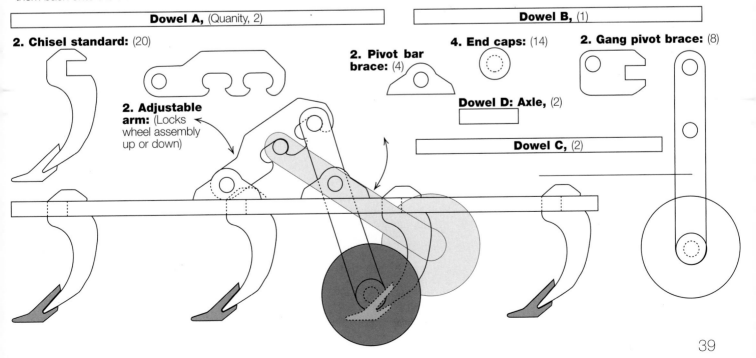

Dowel A, (Quanity, 2)

Dowel B, (1)

2. Chisel standard: (20)

2. Pivot bar brace: (4)

4. End caps: (14)

2. Gang pivot brace: (8)

2. Adjustable arm: (Locks wheel assembly up or down)

Dowel D: Axle, (2)

Dowel C, (2)

The G&H toys

G&H Custom Craft, Davenport, IA has programmed variations of my patterns including the pickup, sports utility and jeep patterns into their CNC router making these toys available in kit form from maple wood. Shown below are models I've put together from the kit and a photo of the kit itself as it would be shipped ready for assembly. The photo below shows each after I glued, sanded and painted them. The pickup is painted with aerosol spray enamel, and sports utility with aerosol automotive metallic lacquer. The jeep is glued, sanded, and assembled with no finish. For painting I used the techniques described on pages 1 and 2. Because the CNC toys don't offer some of the items such as bumpers, roll-bar and hitch, you can make them from the patterns in this book.

At this time G&H is planning to adapt the ag tractor, chisel plow and End-Loader, also from this book.

For information on ordering and other details such as acquiring wheels separately:
Fax: 319-388-5463

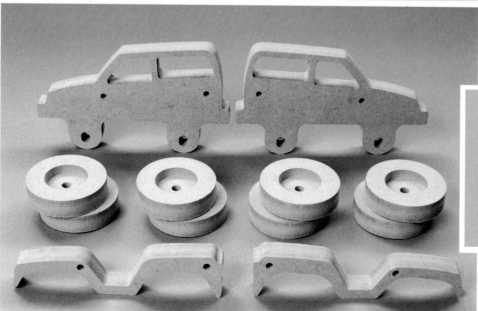

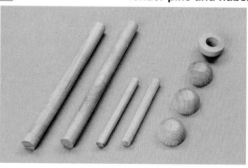

Kit includes axles, fender pins and hubs.

BIOGRAPHY

I feel fortunate to have been an advertising designer for John Deere for thirty four years. I hold a BA in graphic design from The Kansas City Art Institute. My interests have grown through experience working with and photographing machinery combined with demands for simplicity and functional design back at the office.

Over the years I've been intrigued with traditional and modern mediums such as aged pine, exotic woods, oil and acrylic paints, stained glass, plastics, and hard surface material such as Corian® by DuPont®.

Computer experience has enabled me to tackle this latest effort of conceiving, designing, and producing this book featuring my creations.

Of my held and valued possessions, are rights to a registered trademark. **GRRR**® RAVES

MY FRIEND JOHN (cover photo)

John Kerr is my neighbor. To me, he is the perfect model to complement my toy designs. His genuine youthful excitement brings to mind those days many years ago when I was growing up on the Graves family farm. My few precious toys stood in grand reverence in the fresh, cool soil on a favorite spot under an old elm. Over tiny fields with fences of sticks and strings, day dreams abounded as I gazed up with wonder at the "Kansas in August" heat rippling and distorting the horizon into a great mirage of green and gold. Time seemed to stand still. And then, with a blink, forty-some years raced into memory. That feeling of youthful excitement still abounds in my shop while creating a toy. I hope John enjoys playing with his truck as I would have many years ago, and I also hope that you recall precious memories of early years while creating a toy.

This book is dedicated to my Mom, Almeda, for her lifetime dedication and encouragement to her family and for urging me into a life of art. And to my loving wife Mary who surrenders me to many hours in the shop.